"Once a good girl's gone bad, she's gone forever, I'll mourn forever..."

JAY-Z, FROM "SONG CRY"

But, if she's born bad, can she get better? Can she change her life forever?

AALIYAH "A$AP" PERSON

TABLE OF CONTENTS

Prologue	1
The Forgotten	2
When I Look In The Mirror…	4
To Harm Or To Heal	5
When The Glue Is Removed	6
The Truth Of The Matter Is This	7
Get Ready	8
Unity	9
Tears, Boo'd Up Remix	10
Runaway Girl	11
True	12
Suicide's Victims	13
Forgiveness	14
5 Words Poem, Words & Letters	15
Butterflies	16
Anxiety	17
More Or Less	18
Pearly Gates	19
Sunrise Symphony	20
To My Twin Daughters	21
The Fixer	22
Imagine If…	23
Transcending Walls	24
Flowers & Feathers	25
Freedom Isn't Free	26
Epilogue	27

PROLOGUE

I collected some of my poems from my recent 10 year vacation at the luxurious CCWF and CIW women's state institutions. All meals, bedding, clothing, and trauma was inclusive. I'm glad I left before the COVID-19 Pandemic lockdowns and the pandemonium that followed with CDCR allowing its visitors to self-identify their gender under SB 132. I was sad to leave all of the friends that I made during my stay behind. But, like the CCWF Receiving Yard Captain said when I entered CDCR, "You come here by yourself, you leave by yourself. Don't forget that." No offense to those males who identify as trans, who still have their working parts, but this is a nightmare for the nearly 90% of women who are already serving long sentences because of men, further adding to the inhumanity and trauma of these institutions who lie to society and say that they are rehabilitating people. But, I digress.

I have also added some post-incarceration poems, which I have recently composed. My thoughts, beliefs, and reflections of the past decade, as well as the present climate, spill out in my poetry, like waterfalls over a cliff. I love writing poems, oration of them aloud is another story. I'm improving on this skill for myself in order to regain the confidence that I lost to the injustice system. I pray you enjoy these poems as well as the insightful dialogue of their origins. I am humbly grateful to My Creator, my family, and my handful of friends who have supported me and my vision along my journey of transformation from pain to power. I would name you all, but I don't want to forget anyone. You know who you are if you're reading this.

So, without further ado, I thank you.

And to the rest who are just reading this without knowing me, thank you for taking the chance to learn something new and to gain some wisdom along the way!

Enjoy!

THE FORGOTTEN

LEFT-----

BEHIND COLD CONCRETE----

THROWN A TRAY OF SCRAPS TO EAT.

SILENCED, IN STRIPES,

SCREAM, ONLY A FEW HEAR MY CRIES---

NO ONE CARES.

LIES IN THEIR SMILES,

THE DEVIL IN THEIR EYES.

LOCKED-DOWN----

23-HOURS A DAY----

HEARTBEATS ECHO,

BUT MINE TURNED COLD TODAY.

I BECAME ONE OF "THEM"-----

PRESUMED GUILTY BEFORE MY PLEA----

I'M #1201438:

PERSON, AALIYAH SOLANGE ALI

PLEASE----

DON'T FORGET ABOUT ME!!!!!

SCREAMIN': "NOT GUILTY!" 'TIL I D-I-E!!!!

This poem was the first thing I wrote after I was remanded in court at my arraignment on February 16, 2012. After waiting in the freezing cold holding tank for over 20 hours, I was finally housed in lock-down because of my charges. It was loud, it smelled badly, and it was eerily echoing. And the vibe was dark and sterile. I met a girl who I would later be roommates with at Chowchilla that day in the holding tank. I couldn't use the restroom in front of everyone. Privacy was violated through basic needs and strip searches. Ironically, I was bleeding from having a miscarriage due to how I was arrested on the 8th of February. I bled for six months straight and still had positive preganancy tests at medical, until I complained to the Grievance Hotline, and they rushed me out to the hospital, which was merely across the parking lot. County Jail is a horrendous place, made worse by its employees who take their position of power over other humans too seriously. It's sickening. The food, the clothes, the smells, the filth, the power trips, and cruelty are overall not a conducive environment to receive a fair trial, let alone be treated humanely. But, that's all in its grand design. So, I guess it's doing exactly what they designed it to do: to break people down to control them and keep populations segregated, isolated, weak, and repressed. I would not wish jail or prison as a place of punishment for my worst enemy. There are much better ways to restore justice.

When I Look In The Mirror, What Do I See?

I see someone who does not fit the pofile for three felonies.

I see someone whose innocence was taken before her teens.

I see a child of divorced parents who grew up too fast.

I see a woman of God with a tattered past.

I see someone who has the potential to be great again.

I see an educated mother of female twins.

I see a diamond shining just under that layer of coal.

I see a great friend with open arms whose heart was once so cold.

I see a woman unafraid to conquer her fears.

I see a beautiful face who shouldn't cry so many tears.

I see metamorhisis happening right before my eyes.

I see my cocoon transforming into a butterfly.

I see a dreamer who now has the knowledge and strength she needs.

I see a giver who is kind to everyone she meets.

I see a person who now heals instead of causing destruction.

I see my determination to reach goals without interruption.

I see a positive change in my own mediated self-reflection.

I see I am the boss of my own deliberate, purposeful direction.

When I look in the mirror, what do I see?

I see a powerful force who can be anything she chooses to be.

I see a vigorous might who has decided her future destiny to succeed.

I wrote this poem when I was housed at CIW, after five years into my sentence. I was working in the Education Department and going to college. I was already done with my AD-SEG/SHU stint by then. The Principal posted a poetry contest with the prompt similar to the title: "When You Look In the Mirror, What Do You See?" The only requirements were to keep it under one page. I won a much-coveted "free-world" water bottle and the opportunity to read my poem aloud in front of an assembly of my peers and The Warden. I turned five shades of red that day. It was empowering to read this to my peers that day. It was also a transformative moment for me, reminding me that I can do anything I put my mind to, that I matter, and I can make a difference with my words.

TO HARM OR TO HEAL

To harm or to heal...
God gave us two hands:
To harm or to heal.
To harm or to heal?
I'mma keep it oh so real---
To help someone up or to wield the steel?
A slap and a fist or a hug and a kiss?
A mean mug and a sign or a smile with the peace sign?
Freedom and Life, in a flash, can be taken away,
By decisions and choices that are hastily made.
We must logically think before becoming enslaved,
Or sent to meet our Maker from an early grave.
Think about it before it's too late.
To harm or to heal?
To heal or to harm?
Don't be alarmed--
Make the best choice with your two hands at the end of your arms.

I wrote this poem at CIW when I was thinking about alternative outcomes of my case. I was initally so angry at the entire situation because I was really trying to be a peacemaker between my "Victim" and my friend. In retrospect, I know now not to get involved in domestic situations of other people's relationships. But, back then, I just didn't want my friend to return to prison for another senseless murder. I consciously made a decision prior to my release that I would not seek revenge. I would forgive my "Victim" for making a mistake of lying to the courts and police about me, and that I would not kill her for snitching. Does this make me a punk? No. This makes me wiser because I refuse to give energy to the negative things that have happened to me in my life. I acknowledge them. I learn from them. And, I grow, moving forward into a better, healed person from them.

WHEN THE GLUE IS REMOVED

What do you do when they remove the glue?

The GLUE, the mother, that holds the family together...

Who's gonna brush the kids' hair and tie their shoes?

Who's gonna take them to school?

Juggling five tasks with one body as if she has elastic, octopus arms,

Multiple generations are collectively connected,

Instantly, like electricity, with calls, texts, emails, and cards,

Keeping the social aspect of society alive,

Adding flavor and spice to lives,

With hugs, handshakes, smiles, love, encouragement, and high fives.

When the glue is removed,

Children become sad,

Food becomes bland,

No more fun trips to the beach to play in the sand.

The garden and the family wither in despair.

All because the glue is no longer there.

This poem was written when I spoke at a Santa Cruz County JAG (Justice and Gender) Meeting, as a Special Guest Speaker, on a plenary panel about women's issues faced in incaceration. This was my introduction to explain why mothers are so important in our communities and why locking them up does nothing but hurt the familial unit, further fragmenting our already dysfunctional society. Unfortunately, one of the members of that meeting was still stuck on my charges, wrote bad press about it, did not acknowledge that I was, am, and will always be a mother, despite the fact that I already served time for crimes I did not commit and endured subhumane treatment inside. We have got to do better as humans.

THE TRUTH OF THE MATTER IS THIS

I'm from the land of thugs, slugs, and drugs;
mean mugs worn like your daily attire,
and the money from the buyers only gettin' sellers higher.
Trying to get a sliver of a better Bayview,
Stacking people on top of people like the coroners do,
gentrification pushing the real out the hood for a bigger revenues on the avenues.
Now let's review:
Justice will never truly be served if those serving peace do it with a loaded piece. (REPEAT)
When will all the killing cease?
When we are all deceased?
When we cross the line?
and end up be-hind
vertical lines, called bars, on cages?
This situation is getting outrageous!
Would you really put your own children in cages?
When will all this suffering cease?
Maybe when we learn to treat strangers
better than
our Family or friends...
When we stop pretending that those holding the most dividends
don't always set trends,
And those committing the biggest crimes against men & women
are, more often than not,
overlooked and not caught.
Systemic failure
deeply rooted in
insecure transgressions,
causing permanent impressions
and generational depressions.
Are you getting the suggestion?
I've got far too many unanswered questions
about WHY this gets LESS attention.
My message to you,
it's just a cumulative life lesson,
to seek out the truth:
The truth of the matter is this:
We must act accordingly, locally and logically,
to make our ancestors happy
to see
that we—yes, we,
you and you and you and me—
are FINALLY FREE!!!
F-R-E-E (free)(gratis)
and at peace,
In unity with one another...
Until our paths cross again, I give you and leave you with:
Peace.

GET READY

GET READY
GET READY!
'Cuz I'm goin places
Doin' Things,
Watch out for what my future brings!

On your mark, get ready, set, go
A$AP on the scene
Stompin in my Steeltoes
Fresh out the pen
From over ten
Years, know---
I ain't playin---
These hoes wanna get paid and tell,
Oh, well,
Now I'm deaf to the static
Can't hear what they're sayin!
So, swell
It ain't my fault
I'm still ballin'
While they still crawlin'---
I stay winnin' and grinnin'
While they're chasin' crumbs and sinnin'!
That bum still ain't got shiiiiiiit---
I got an excuse,
But still came out ahead of you,
Booooooo!
Boo-who...boo, who????
Move out of my face---
I may forgive,
But your actions, I can never erase.
I just try to replace
Them with better ones,
'Cuz I am the CHAMPION!!!!!

UNITY

United we stand
Divided we fall
We gotta stand tall
And learn to walk
After we crawl
We gotta get up
And fight the good fight
We gotta work together
All Day & All Night.

TEARS

Tears fall down my face,
Landing on my shirt.
I know PAIN.
I feel when it HURTS.
It's bad enough being here;
I don't want it to be worse, living in fear.
Never look a gift horse in the mouth,
Nor cross in front of a moving hurst.
The tears dry and the pain goes away.
I'd rather cry tears of joy than pain any day.

Boo'd Up Remix

If it weren't for dark times,
Your star couldn't shine!
Contemplating August 21, 19-99,
The first day
You and your twin became mine.
Wish I could do what you did,
Nicknamed: "The Comeback Kid."
Once I finish my state bid,
My Comeback Stage can begin.
I once chose friends over family.
Now, it's all family, no friends.
Sittin' in my 6 by 9,
Waitin' on ten to end.
Promisin' to make it (uh-huh),
By any means.
Given a chance,
I'm gon' take it,
Got a pocket full of dreams.
Starin' at cell walls,
Made of cold concrete.
Future plans lookin' grand.
Can you hear my heartbeat go: Bah'd up, boo'd up,
Baby, Bad'h up, boo'd up?!

Runaway Girl

Runaway, Girl----
They're fast on your heels.
Over the wooden fences
And metal gates,
Landing into a yard
With a dog barking &
Trying to bite you;
Over another fence,
Trying not to get cut
By broken glass and razor wires,
Into the arms of someone
Whose idea of LOVE is attached to
22-inch rims on scrapers
And Dead President Papers.
Hugs & Slugs.
Kisses & Kicks.
No one in this world deserves
Treatment like this.
So, keep running, Girl,
Keep dodging your death,
Run, run, run----
Until you run out of breath.

This poem was inspired by the book, "Runaway Girl" by Carissa Phelps. This is not a summarizing poem of that book, but rather it was an interpretation of the title juxtaposed with my personal life experiences.

TRUE

Fake, false, unreal, untrue--
Are these descriptions of
What I REALLY am to you?
If you're through,
Then, be through.
And, if you're TRUE,
Then, be TRUE.
I wish I could fix everyone
Who's broken with glue.
Then, I could EASILY
Fix you.
But who's really there?
Who really cares?
A real bitch,
A beautiful Queen,
Down for you from the start.
I can only apologize
For what those previous girls did
To your heart---
And your soul.
But, G-O-D can help make you whole
And help heal the hole
You have inside you,
So, you can clearly see,
Without glasses,
Who's really REAL & TRUE.
And, that's ME for YOU!
And, YOU for ME!
T-R-U-E:
The Real Understand Everything!

Suicide's Victims

**She didn't have to go out that way.
She didn't have to die.
Another incarcerated mother tossed away,
Another soul lost to suicide.**

**Growing like the waves in the ocean,
Growing stronger with high tide.
Washing away yesterday's pain like a potion,
Washing away numbers who died by suicide.**

**Of all the days I've been here—
Of all the days I have left to go—
It is a mysterious, tragic reminder.
It remains enigmatic why CIW suicide stats still grow.**

**Could we pay better attention to warning signs?
Could we have saved one, maybe two?
Anyone, who is burdened with hard times,
Anyone saved before her lips turned BLUE.**

RIP SHAYLENE "BLUE: GRAVES: 6-1-2016 (bottom pic) & ERIKA ROCHA: 4-14-2016 (top pic). This poem was written in 2014 a month after I arrived at CIW. That year, there were 14 attempted suicides by March of 2014. The combination of depression, anxiety, and the availability of drugs in prison all led to this spike in suicides. I knew two of the women who actually died by suicide in the first few months of my arrival at CIW. While the number of attempted and completed suicides did decrease over the remainder of time I was there, the number of women who still struggle with mental health disorders has remained fairly constant. I also knew one of the women who did not die by suicide, but rather by homicide when her girlfriend killed her and made it look like suicide in 2016. Shaylene "Blue" Graves. CDCR reported she died by suicide. Ironically, I was in SHU at the time. Everyone of us back there knew about the murder right after it happened because we got calls from the women in Harrison A & B, and notified her mother about the incident on our cell phones before the prison did. We were raided shortly after that by all of the ISU (Institutional Security Units) from the 6 nearby prisons that next day. Suicide is a direct result of the lack of mental health care and attention by others when people feel hopeless & helpless, both in and out of prison. If you know someone struggling with hopeless and helpless ideations, please call the hotline 1-800-273-TALK (8255), 988 on cell phones, or seek out help from friends or professionals.

FORGIVENESS

I know if God can forgive her,
I can too.
The old me would've beat her black & blue.
How could she?
Take the stand on me,
After I intervened,
Trying to keep the peace
And keep my brother free.
I would never have done that to you:
Raise my hand and tell lies that aren't true,
Especially because she knew
That I took care of two plus two.
Whew!
Forever more I need to
Let it go
And move on to
A bigger future.
I know if God can forgive her,
I can too.
The old me would've beat her black & blue.

This poem was written as a way to release the pain I held onto as a result of my case. It was painful because I was playing the peacemaker in the middle of a domestic situation, which I should not have been involved in. Hard lesson learned though. I learned how to forgive people of their shortcomings and faults. I was also angry from being ripped away from my family, especially my twins, as well as from miscarrying my unborn child. Scientific studies have shown that the energy required to get upset causes all sorts of negative effects on personal health, so I would rather remain at peace and be healthy by expressing my feelings, getting it out, letting it go, healing, and moving on with my life.

5 WORDS POEM

TRUTH * STRENGTH * HUGE * LOVE * PAIN

THE TRUITH OF OUR STRENGTH
COMES FROM GREAT LENGTHS
OF HUGE LOVE AND PAIN
WITH OR WITHOUT GAIN
TO BE TRUE IS TO BE YOU
THE REAL YOU
NOT WHO SOMEONE THINKS YOU ARE.
FOR, EVERYONE WAS BORN A STAR
AND EVERYONE NEEDS TO KNOW THAT
THE TRUTH IS TO LOVE YOURSELF
TO HEAL THE PAIN.

WORDS & LETTERS

They say: "Sticks and stones may break my bones,
But words will never hurt me."
This saying seems untrue
Because some words form knives
That cut
Right through
My heart and my gut
Causing me to send out hurtful words and letters I may not mean
Right to my *corazon*.
Now, he's pushed me away,
And threw his brick wall back up,
Leaving me alone in isolation.
You can't take back what's been said once it's spoken
With more words and letters
Assembled together.
So, how do we start to mend our hearts once they're broken?

BUTTERFLIES

A Poem To My Mom After
My Grandma Lorraine Passed On

Let the fluttering wings of these butterflies
Lift you and surround you with love
Like the angels in heavenly skies
And our GOD, who is above.
Although your mom has passed on,
Know she's in a better place.
Although she's physically gone,
Her memory will never be erased.

This was the hardest period of my prison sentence: the passing of my Grandmother Lorraine. "Bama" was the childhood nickname I gave to her. She was an activist, a teacher, the 2012 CA State Congressional "Woman of The Year," and would have been 100 this year. This woman was mothering, humorous, educated, tenacious, relentless, always had a smile on her face and candy in her purse. She loved when I sang her songs from "Annie" at the top of my lungs in her car, especially "The Sun Will Come Out Tomorrow." She passed in 2016 after I was released from AD-SEG/SHU. I couldn't go to her funeral for two reasons: I was in CIW (Corona) and my custody levels were too high to be transported. I was devastated. I still haven't fully grieved her loss, but I visited her gravesite and saw a butterly and a rabbit circling her grave. She was there, hugging me. I felt it.

ANXIETY

Heartbeats racing
Walls are closing in all around
Mouth is dry like cotton
Palms drip with sweat
Gasping
Trying to catch my breath
Trying to speak
But words are trapped
No escaping
From inside my head
Pounding
Can't concentrate
Light is too bright
Paralyzed
Don't want to move
Stuck
Just want to
Be able to
Be able
To be normal
To breathe
And see
And think
And function again

MORE OR LESS

In life, I've learned that less is more:

Less sleep, more energy.

Less food, more movement.

Less friends, more productivity.

Less money, more motivation.

Less materials, more peace.

It's the simplest things that bring the most happiness.

My kids were happier with the boxes on holidays than what came inside them.

So, why does society push us to do more?

More work, less pay.

More bills, less time.

More movement, less energy.

More hate, less love.

More materials, less happiness.

This is a recipe for disaster,

For pulling a society and tribe apart at the seams,

And leaving the ones who lose everything, including themselves,

Scattered like trash along the edges of cities and towns.

So, is it better to have more or less?

I'll stay humbled and blessed with less.

Pearly Gates

I may fall down seven times, but stand up eight, Prayed and wait until the day I see the pearly gates, Streets paved with gold and beautiful riches untold, Gardens with all kinds of fruits unknown, under which rivers flow. A place where the energies and love are bright and light, where fear and bad intentions don't exist because they're not right. I have got some sins, which I've asked to be forgiven. I wonder if I will still make it in to Heaven? I wonder if anyone gets left outside the pearly gates. I wonder if there is a line where the mostly decent people are made to agonizingly wait, while their overall life and deeds get analyzed. I wonder if the angels can tell just by looking deep in someone's eyes. Of all the things I look forward to, in this short life I live, I wonder will it all be worth it, when I get to go to "God's Crib." But I can't call it a "crib" because God has always existed. Maybe I should call it: "God's Spot" in case there is a place, other than Earth, where His Creation were all admitted. I just know I have always been told and taught that I should be good to go there. What if the gates are not pearly when I get there? Will I be aware of where I am at? Or will I run the other way because I am afraid of the fallen Angel whose roads are paved with flames?

Sunrise Symphony

How beautiful the sound
Birds chirping all around
Back and forth
As if being conducted
By Allah (swt)
On cue, they pause
One second, two,
For the grand entrance
of the Sun from the East
They wind up again,
Every note a part of the
Grand Melody
All perfectly blend
As if from a symphony
then, the wind chimes in
It's soft breeze
Making a swooshing noise
Gently dancing, dodging branches
Through the trees and leaves
Dust particles sparkle and dance
Through the new light
Like glitter from Heaven
Moving to the sound
Slow then fast
Rhythmically synchronized in Allah's Lovely Orchestra.

TO MY TWIN DAUGHTERS

I remember, in the beginning,
When they told me, "There are 2!"
I could hardly go to sleep,
Just trying to picture you.
Then, they told me you were 2 boys.
And, then, a boy and a girl.
All I cared about was that you were healthy,
The center of my world!
On August 21st,
My doctor said, "Congrats, they're 2 girls!"
I took a sigh of relief,
Then cried a tear of joy.
For, you were both healthy;
And, I'm glad you were not boys!
I've watched you grow into young ladies,
So proper and so poised.
Each with your own identity,
Never afraid to make a joyful noise!
And, as you go into the world,
Venturing off to be what you want to be,
Know that I support and love you.
I just want you to succeed!
Be smart and confident
With every decision that you choose.
And, as long as we have each other and God,
We can never lose!
Spread your wings, my twin butterflies;
It's now your turn to shine!
And no matter what you do,
I'm always proud that you are mine!

                        Love Always,
                             Mom

THE FIXER

Why do I
Continually look for love?
I think I have found it!
No! Wait!
He pushed me away;
He's too busy
Saving the World,
Flirting with girls,
Grabbing my neck,
Pulling my curls,
Cuddling,
Creating puddles,
Pulling me closer at night
Under heavy blankets,
Holding me tight,
Flip-flopping,
Tossing,
Wait, hold me there---
How I get bubble guts,
Or, are they butterflies,
At the very thought of him.
He fits perfectly
Next to, around, inside of me.
Why? No, really, why?
He's the greatest guy,
My King!
Or, is he?
Or, is he the devil in disguise?
Does he yearn for the success
Like I? Like me...
I pull the stress out of his body
With deep massages
From his hips to his feet,
From his back, shoulders, and neck,
Out of his fingers,
From his waist
With my tongue,
My Bay, baby, babe.
We're up late,
Up early
Forever Young
Is he my forever?
My last stop?
Well, It's been a long while
Since I last stopped--
Like 12 years, so...
I don't know,
If this is where I grab tight
And hold on for my life---
Or, if I should get off,
And let go
Before my heart and mind
Entwine their roots
Into an ideal,
Giving me something to feel
Because my body and soul
Are already gone.
If he was a drug,
I'd already be hooked,
Looking to be fixed,
Everytime the high of our love came down,
I just don't want to drown,
But I do
Want him around.
I don't want to fail,
But I feel like I'm flailing, falling, floating.
I don't want this feeling
Of euphoria to ever end.
Infinite love from the Fixer.

iMaCiNe iF...

Imagine if there were no prisons...
Imagine if everyone was free...
Imagine if there was no currency...
Would they still be able to control the community?

Imagine if we loved more than hated...
Imagine if nothing was gated...
Imagine if there were no borders...
Would the world have many less disorders?

Imagine if travel accommodations were free...
Imagine if you loved me for me, not just what you see...
Imagine if there was less pollution...
Would this help with the crime solution?

Imagine if we all gave...
Imagine if there were never slaves...
Imagine if there was no vanity...
Would we be better as a healed humanity?

Imagine if materialism ended...
Imagine if the wealth inequities were upended...
Imagine if everyone had a great education...
Would this be a better nation without incarceration?

#ENDMASSINCARCERATION #EDUCATIONNOTINCARCERATION #TIMEBACK
#SCHOOLSNOTPRISONS #IMAGINEDIFFERENTALTERNATIVESTOPRISON
I'm sure there are more hashtags, but you get the jist of it. We need a better solution. The systems in place are antiquated, outdated, unfair, racist, and slated in the wrong direction for protection, growth, and healing of humanity.

TRANSCENDING WALLS

***Maya Angelou, one of my greatest inspirations, once wrote, "Love recognizes no barriers. It jumps hurdles, leaps fences, penetrates walls to arrive at its destination, full of hope."
(This poem is inspired by her quote.)

Love transcends prison walls
Where death and turmoil calls.
In sunshine, spring flowers bloom
Where a shank can lead to your doom.
Butterflies fly in fresh air
Where we must constantly be aware.
Smells of dairies nearby
Where there are sounds of fights and cries.
Trees give shade to the yard
Where we must remain on guard.
Beautiful faces glow on femmes and studs
Where you can hang with the crips or the bloods.
Birds make a collective joyful noise
Where you can get hemmed up by "them boys."
Grasses wet with fresh morning dew
Where you can get beat black and blue.
Soft sheets allow sleep and comatoses
Where fentanyl causes overdoses.
Love transcends prison walls
Where death and turmoil calls.

The reality in prison is that you may not make it home. There have been an increasing number of drug overdoses because of Fentanyl, especially in prison. Many struggle with depression, anger issues, grief, loss, and are burdened with being forced to be in hostile situations, which can become increasing violent very quickly. Gangs, drugs, mental health issues, and same-sex relationships in prison along with the rules and design of the institution itself are not conducive to a safe environment to just "do your time and go home." I witnessed brutal beatings, fights, riots, murder, overdoses, and abuse of all kinds while I was at both Chowchilla and CIW (CDCR). These are not places I would send my worst enemies, let alone people I cared for and wanted to see change. I work daily to shut these institutions down. They are hell on Earth in my opinion. Anyone who supports them should stay a week there as a resident, then talk to me about your opinions.

Flowers & Feathers

They say to give people their flowers
To let them know they are appreciated,
To let them know you love them.
On the holidays, weddings and funerals, I see the most flowers.
I love them because they are bright and colorful.
They are adornments scattered about for our enjoyment
Like a little smile on a stick
Flowers after picked, eventually wilt and die.
But in prison, that was what helped my days pass by:
The hope of seeing color outside in patches on the way to the chow hall.
Prison, where everything was dulled and monotoned,
Lifeless, depressed, and drained,
I always dreamt of flowers and feathers.
Flowers to brighten my day,
And feathers so I could be like a hawk and fly away.
Like the red-tailed hawk that follows me everywhere I go,
Form coast to coast,
From prison to freedom.
Be sure to give people their flowers while they are here,
But, don't forget the feathers, too.
So they can fly freely and enjoy the splashes of color from a bird's eye view.

I read this poem on a plenary panel at College Nine at UCSC on October 14, 2022. I was on the panel for Tim Fitzpatrick's class with Dr. John Brown Childs, Daniel "Nane" Alejandrez, and former lifers Henry Frank and Frankie Alejandrez. The topic of discussion was reimagining incarceration. We have a long way to go in this country with the "injustice system" design until we reach Norway's model. However, these open discussions and talks engage the youth and stimulate the minds of tomorrow's future leaders, who potentially will have a hand in making greater changes to these repressive systems. Thank you to all of the UCSC Staff and Students who listened and actively participated in this discussion.

Freedom Isn't Free

Freedom Isn't Free,
From sea to shining sea,
What losing my freedom cost me
Can't even be bought for a fee.

I lost my unborn son, my kids, my house, and my cars,
And beyond all the material stuff, I lost my dignity behind bars.
I lost my confidence and morality
With the turn of those jail keys.

Confining me to be
In a place where I had even lost me.
But, that was only temporary.
Thank G-O-D.

Because nothing I did was worth any received punishment.
And nothing I saw nor endured equated time or money well spent.
Those who created and believe in this system
Better run and repent before it comes around to get them.

The cost of freedom should have no price,
But daily there are soldiers whose lives are sacrificed
In the streets and in the military, equally.
To my brother, I am truly sorry.
The system was designed to conquer and divide unity.
I can only reveal what I have lived and see.
Quite simply: Freedom Isn't Free.

EPILOGUE

If you made it this far, this is the not the end of my journey, but the end of this book. I appreciate you. Thank you for purchasing and reading my works of poetry. I am interested to hear the feedback from my peers and audience. This took a great deal emotionally, spiritually, and physically for me to compile, since I lost the majority of my written works in 2020. But, I feel accomplished to have created, compiled, and completed this. It was a true labor of love, pain, and power. I found some copies of my lost works in the letters I had written home to my daughters and mother. In addition, reading through these poems, both old and new, as well as the commentary, I feel I have achieved my goal of sharing my authentic, real-life experiences by expressing painful to freeing moments of my journey. I am excited to announce that I will be writing more soon. I have a book-to-movie transcript in the works. Stay tuned. Stay blessed. Stay out of the way and on your way to be great. It's never too late. Whatever your dreams or goals, remember: if you thought of the idea, you can make it happen! You can do it! I promise you this.

Peace, Prosperity, and Positivity,

Made in the USA
Columbia, SC
19 May 2025